ALLEN PHOT

C000133517

THE GERMAN SHEPHERD DOG

CONTENTS

INTRODUCTION

The German Shepherd Dog is included in the Kennel Club's Pastoral group because the breed was originally used to herd and guard sheep. The herding breeds are highly intelligent and very trainable and this is especially true of German Shepherd Dogs who can be used for a wide variety of work.

As family and companion dogs they will need firm but kind owners to develop their full character which is to be alert, self-assured and tractable. They are of a suitable size for a house dog, have easily managed coats and a life expectancy of about twelve years.

It is their unique blend of intelligence, beauty and fluid movement that makes them so popular.

Adult dog

Adult bitch

Bronze statue by Arno Zauche (1923) of a winning dog in Germany and America

HISTORY

GERMANY

The German Shepherd dog was developed as a recognised breed just over a century ago. It evolved from working dogs descended from those that tended sheep for hundreds of years, herding the flocks to the unfenced pastures, keeping them there and, in earlier times, guarding them from wolves and predators. It was almost entirely due to the foresight of Rittmeister von Stephanitz, who saw their potential for other work, that the breed was started. With other interested people, a standard was drawn up and a club formed to further the development of a dog that could work in other ways than just with sheep. This club, the Verein für Deutsche Schäferhunde (SV), is still active today to control the breed. The dogs soon became popular in Germany and, although it was for work that the breed was developed, their attractive appearance and flowing gait as well as their intelligence and loyalty to their owners, helped them to become popular worldwide.

BRITAIN

After being seen working with the German troops in the First World War, some dogs were imported into Britain soon after the end of the War. When a breed club was formed in 1919, they were called Alsatians, as some had come from Alsace, rather than the unpopular term 'German'. They soon became popular here, too popular; to meet

PAT dogs; the puppy started visiting at seven weeks and qualified in six months

the demand, poor specimens were bred without the correct temperament. Numbers fell and the Second World War caused more culling (because people could not afford to feed their dogs) but the good work they did with the Forces made sure that they regained their popularity after the War. This time more care was taken by breeders and societies to maintain their good image. The breed is now fully accepted as a working one which makes a reliable family and companion dog for those who make sure that they get a well-bred and carefully reared puppy and have the time to undertake a correct upbringing. The name of the breed was changed to German Shepherd Dog in 1977 and although 'Alsatian' is still in common use, it is the same breed whichever name is used.

Although registered as pastoral dogs they will be found working with the police, the Forces, Search and Rescue, as Guide Dogs for the Blind and as registered PAT (Pets for Therapy) dogs visiting the sick and elderly in hospitals and homes.

Guide Dog for the Blind

BREED STANDARD

This defines what is required, both mentally and physically, for the German Shepherd Dog to carry out the necessary work. They are medium- to large-sized dogs, slightly longer in body than height (to enable them to keep on the trot for a long time), well-balanced, free from exaggerated movement, but with fore and aft angulation in the shoulder and hock necessary to produce a far-reaching, effortless and tireless gait. In temperament they must be courageous, steady, resilient and tractable, never nervous, shy or aggressive. The herding and guarding work ingrained in them means that they have the ability to be a defensive guard when necessary but friendly and gentle when off duty.

Movement – the extended trot

They have erect ears and a weatherproof coat and, whilst they are of an attractive appearance, working ability must never be sacrificed to beauty and as a working breed they will need regular daily exercise whatever the weather.

BUYING A GERMAN SHEPHERD DOG

Buying a puppy is the best way to start as an older dog may have already learnt bad habits or, if kennel-reared, may not have been socialised.

German Shepherd Dogs need to be part of family life from an early age. They do not do well kept in large numbers in kennels. A puppy of this breed learns very quickly and will adapt to your routine.

Never buy unseen from an advertisement. Try to get a recommendation to an experienced and reliable breeder but remember it is likely they will have a waiting list for their puppies as they will only breed a few litters each year. If you want a companion dog, avoid those kennels that specialise in breeding for showing, working or police work. Instead, look for a breeder who, whilst they may show a little, keeps to the standard to produce good-looking, healthy stock but still gives high priority to breeding for the temperament suitable for family dogs. Although the German Shepherd Dog is a healthy breed, all breeds have hereditary faults and any which are likely to occur should be known to breeders who should have studied the pedigrees and history of their breeding stock.

BREEDERS' RESPONSIBILITIES

The caring breeder will want to make sure that you are able to give the puppy the attention he needs, have the time to train the growing youngster, give the adult dog sufficient exercise and that at no time will the dog be left alone all day. Also, if you have young children then you may be advised to wait until they can learn how to treat a puppy.

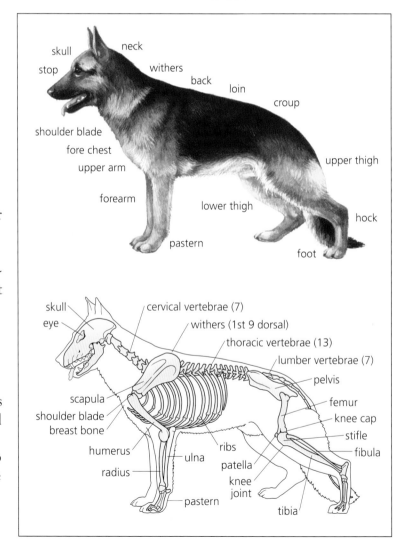

Bitch with her two-week-old puppies

For your part you must check that both parents have been X-rayed for hip dysplasia and have low scores. Hip dysplasia is defined as hip joints with incorrect formation. Although partly hereditary, feeding and environment are involved. All breeding stock should be X-rayed and the plates scored by a panel of scrutineers at the British Veterinary Association. The BVA will use a scoring system of between 0 and 53 for each hip. The average for the breed is a total of 18 and the results are published by the Kennel Club. If both parents have been X-rayed and have low scores it should not be necessary to X-ray a companion dog but the condition can only be confirmed by an X-ray, not by looking at the movement of the dog.

Check that the puppy will be registered with the Kennel Club and that the transfer of ownership will be ready when you collect him. With the transfer you should get six weeks free health insurance and the option to extend it for a year. This should be considered and continued if felt necessary but third party insurance should be maintained for life. The puppy may be tattooed for identification but, if not, this can be done later as can the insertion of a microchip if you do not mind a foreign body being implanted in the dog.

Typical two-week-old puppy

Finally, the breeder should be prepared to give 'after-sales advice' and want to know of the progress of the puppy.

So, if you are satisfied but there is not a litter available, book a puppy and wait. You should not be asked for a deposit until the litter is born and there is a puppy suitable for you.

Puppies at four weeks

Three-and-a-half-week old sable puppy

CHOICE OF PUPPY

Whether to have a dog or bitch is a matter of personal choice. Bitches are slightly smaller and can be easier to train. They do not need to be bred from and can be spayed if it is felt necessary but not until they are well over a year old. A dog will need a firm hand while he is growing on from nine to eighteen months but, once he is an adult, will be as easy to manage as a bitch. Male German Shepherd Dogs should not need to be castrated but those kept as pets should not be used at stud.

Six-week-old puppies

Colour, again, is a personal choice but note that, with the black and golds (whatever shade), the black will recede to possibly only a black saddle and some markings so that they will look lighter when adult. All-blacks and bi-colours will stay the same. Bi-colours are rare these days but the breeder can show you any available. The sables, who must have at least one parent this colouring, will look darker when

Black and gold markings

Sable

All black

they grow their adult coat. Any of these colours are accepted for showing but all-whites are not. They can be registered and make suitable companions if carefully bred and reared but should not be crossed with colours.

The coat of the German Shepherd Dog should be smooth and neither too long nor too short but with a close undercoat for resistance to cold. In full coat there can be a form of ruff and slight trousering in the adult. Long-coated puppies can be picked out at seven weeks. These are throwbacks, not a variety and they are not considered for showing as they can lack the necessary undercoat but, like the all-whites, they can make good companion dogs and have become popular with those who do not mind the extra grooming needed.

Colour change: (*left*) puppy aged two-and-a-half months and (*right*) the same dog at twenty months

PREPARING FOR THE PUPPY

You will be given a diet sheet by the breeder so that you can get in supplies. You also want to find a local veterinary surgeon so you can continue any inoculation programme started by the breeder. Discuss this fully with the vet because there is concern that too much can be given too soon before the puppy's immune system has developed, thus leading to problems later. If, therefore, you require other protection such as homoeopathic nosodes and other alternative remedies later, then confirm now so that you can be referred to those qualified to provide them. Worming will have been done before purchase and when to worm again included with the diet sheet. Giving garlic as a daily supplement is known to keep down fleas and worms although testing for worm infestation should be undertaken regularly.

You will need feeding bowls, toys to play with and chew, a basket or bed and either a small leather collar or a soft one. A cage or playpen is recommended to start with and a cage is likely to be needed in the car but, even so, a passenger should train the dog to lie quietly in the back and not get out until told to do so. Dogs must never be left in a car in hot weather even for a short time.

Where is the puppy to sleep at night? Leaving the litter to be on his own is very stressful and he should never be expected to sleep alone until well settled in his new home.

Seven-week-old puppy

Litter mates

PUPPY CARE

COLLECTION

Puppies of this breed should be ready to leave the litter by seven to eight weeks old, when they will weigh twelve to fifteen pounds (approx. five-and-a-half to seven kilograms). They will be fully weaned before this but benefit from remaining with the dam and litter up to that age. You should check that the puppy chosen has the correct scissor bite (the correct angle of contact between the upper and lower teeth) and that a male puppy is entire but the breeder should have checked these points before offering the puppies for sale. You should not, however, need to check the temperament if you have made a careful choice of breeder and seen the puppy's parents as all the puppies should be friendly and run up to meet you, they should never run away or hide.

He should not have been fed before travelling and so you should arrive home with a puppy who has not been sick and has likely been asleep most of the way. Let him settle and explore as he wants. He will probably only want a drink and, for a day or so, may not eat the full amounts suggested now that he does not have any competition from his siblings and until he adjusts to the new, strange environment.

(*left*) Puppy at nine weeks and (*right*) a few weeks later

Once settled he will grow fast and his appetite will increase almost daily. Keep to the diet sheet given. His ears will soon become erect although they may go up and down until he has finished teething. He will not need a lot of exercise whilst growing, just short walks and the freedom to run about, play and to sleep when tired.

The breeder will have started socialising the litter and now you should try to accustom him to everything that he is going to meet such as people, children, animals and noises around the home. For a few weeks he will absorb anything new but later will be more aware and have to learn to accept them. It can be difficult to get him out to accustom him to things until the inoculation programme is complete but he can be carried about, have people and children in to meet him and be taken out in the car etc.

The first six months are the most important in the dog's life and he needs good food, attention and training.

The puppies should be outgoing and run to meet you

TRAINING

You train a German Shepherd Dog with your voice; commands are given quietly and firmly to impart to the puppy that you expect to be obeyed which will be reinforced by the praise he gets when he does obey. Any wrongdoing such as a house-training mistake should only be greeted by a disapproving voice which the puppy will soon recognise. Only as a last resort, at any time in his life, should you give punishment other than the tone of your voice and that should be by holding him by the scruff whilst telling him off.

Once you collect the puppy you have started training him, so he must have a name immediately because the way you talk to him is part of his training.

HOUSE TRAINING

This is easy with this breed. Take him out after every meal, when he wakes up or starts looking around urgently and last thing at night. Take him to the same place in the garden, be patient and praise him when he performs. As soon as he understands he will ask to go out and be clean all day and, soon after, at night. Do, however, leave newspapers near the door for a while in case of accidents.

Sit

Drop or flat

BASIC TRAINING

To teach the puppy to **come** when called, wait until he is already coming towards you then call 'name, come' in a happy and encouraging voice, clapping if necessary. Give plenty of praise when he reaches you. Keep this up, gradually getting his attention and calling when he is not looking at you and then finally when he is doing something else. In this case it may be necessary to walk away from him calling to get him started towards you but keep it up until it becomes ingrained in him to come when called throughout his life, whatever he is doing.

Teaching him to **sit** is very easy. Hold something above his head and say 'name, sit' as a short command and at the same time push down on his rear if necessary and

Sit and wait

Sit and stay

Getting used to a lead

then praise him in that position. Do not at this stage use any titbits, praise is sufficient. Having taught the sit you can now use it to prevent the puppy jumping up.

Drop or **flat** is taught by pushing the puppy gently back and down, which can be done whilst he is small and is far better than saying 'sit' first and having to give two commands instead of just 'name, drop'.

Next you will want the puppy to learn to **go to his place or bed**. If you have decided to have a cage you can use it to start this training by saying 'name, place' or 'name, bed' and leave him in there for a short time only. Without a cage he will have to be held there for short periods until he learns. In either case, have his toys there, leave the cage open when not in use so he can get them out, and never use 'place' or 'bed' as punishment.

Introducing a puppy to sheep

Once he learns to sit and drop then it is time to **teach him to remain in that position**. Start with 'name, sit' and then say 'wait', slowly and firmly so that he learns to recognise that there is another command coming. Initially you must wait only a short time and move away from him only a step or two before you call 'name, come', then subsequently increase the distance very slowly so that mistakes do not occur.

Do the same with the **drop** once the 'sit, wait' is learnt. Then you have to change to 'name, stay' which means that the pup stays where he is until you return to him and let him get up. The 'stay'

command has, therefore, to be very firm and, again, learnt very slowly to build up time and distance. Make sure that these two commands are never mixed up to confuse the dog.

Leave, **leave off** or **no** must be part of the training programme, as must teaching bite inhibition from an early age. All puppies bite each other; the bitten one

This ten-week-old puppy is enjoying the agility tunnel

The Kennel Club Good Citizen Dog rosette

cries out and the biter leaves off. So, if your puppy nips you, you must cry out 'ouch' and see that the puppy stops. He usually nips when excited so, to quieten him down, say 'gently' as well and ignore him for a time if necessary. He will soon learn to mouth gently and can then be taught to stop mouthing altogether.

To teach him to **walk on a lead** put a collar on him and let him get used to it before attaching a fairly long lead. Do not let him pull on this, tie him up and let him discover that it is not you he is pulling against but himself. When he has learnt this, he should be able to be walked about on a loose lead.

You can start teaching him to **walk to heel** to your left side when he is coming in to you. Turn just before he reaches you, pat your left leg and say 'heel'. Keep going a short way at a pace that keeps him at heel without him trying to jump up.

GROWING ON

It is very important to keep up the socialising so try to find a 'puppy party' group in your area to attend until the German Shepherd Dog Training Club will accept him. This is not usually before six months which is too late to start with this breed.

Do not let your puppy bark as and when he wants – German Shepherd Dogs are prone to bark at anything strange from an early age if on their own. It is up to you to see that by the time he is an adult he only barks when necessary and stops when told to. It can help to teach him to **speak** when told as well as when to stop because, if he is taught to speak on command he will learn when barking is acceptable and when it is not.

Most German Shepherd Dog training clubs provide domestic training which will enable you to take the Kennel Club's Good Citizen Dog Tests at the dog's appropriate age.

THE ADULT COMPANION DOG

German Shepherd Dogs are not fully mature until nearly three years old for males and turned two for females. They will reach their full size (60 to 65 cm for dogs and 55 to 60 cm for bitches) before these ages but need time to fully develop. Your companion dog will how-ever have settled into your routine and be obedient and suitably trained for life with you, that is, you can take him anywhere and know

Good companions

GSDs enjoy tracking

The scale   The 'A' frame

that he will behave. He will guard you and your property now by barking when necessary at strangers or unusual noises but stop when ordered and of course be friendly towards your friends when you are present.

Care should be taken not to let him get involved when children are playing rough games as he may get too excited and, if other children are present, guard his own family. He will need plenty of exercise now: a long walk whatever the weather. Now that he is fully grown and manageable, learning does not stop. Involve him in all that is going on in the family, give him jobs to do as well as continuing to attend training classes so that he meets other dogs. German Shepherd Dogs love to search for articles, play 'hide and seek' or learn party tricks to show off.

You can continue training for obedience competitions or join a Kennel Club Working Trials Club to train for trials which will involve searching, tracking and jumping. Then there are Kennel Club Agility competitions (rather like showjumping for horses) which can be enjoyed by the dog and is excellent exercise for him.

Long jump   Clear jump

FEEDING AND NUTRITION

The GSD's natural herding instinct to the fore…

Today, as can be seen in any supermarket or dog food store, there is a wide variety of complete foods available which are pleasant to handle and easy to feed straight from the bag according to the maker's instructions, which must be followed. These complete foods are said to be prepared to formulae that provide everything that is needed for the health and growth of the dog from weaning onwards. The ingredients are strictly controlled but even so may contain some that you might not want to use if you saw them. To make the food palatable, artificial flavourings may be added with preservatives, colourings etc.

Dogs are carnivores, that is flesh eaters, as is shown by their teeth which are adapted for tearing not chewing, and by their digestive systems. In the wild they would eat all of the animal killed, the bones and the contents of the stomach as well as the flesh. They would also scavenge for fruit and vegetable matter. Thus they need a diet of meat (or fish) with cereals such as wheat or rice, a little fat, roughage to aid elimination of waste, and water as and when required. Whilst vitamins and minerals should be part of the diet, they may have

Showing off

Round up

to be added to make up for any lost in the preparation of the food.

There are many German Shepherd Dog owners who think that to feed the traditional way – meat and fish with biscuit etc. – is the only way to develop a strong digestion and keep their dogs healthy. It is not so easy as feeding complete foods but can be managed for one or two dogs with a good butcher or pet food store available.

Vitamins, as required, should be from natural sources such as rose hips for vitamin C (although once thought to be manufactured by the dog in sufficient quantity this is

---

DIET FOR EIGHT-WEEK-OLD PUPPY

(not on complete weaning foods)

- **Breakfast** 2 cupfuls milk thickened with baby cereal or similar

- **Lunch and Supper** 8oz (227 g) raw meat cut up very small with a little finely chopped or food processed vegetables (can be cooked to start with)

- **Tea** a small cup of soaked puppy meal moistened with milk. Meal to be soaked first in boiling water and left to cool.

A complete vitamin and mineral supplement should be fed as tablets or powder on food. A drink of milk last thing can be given for a few weeks only, but the above amounts must be gradually increased until by about four months they are doubled as the appetite increases. By six months omit one cereal meal, usually tea, and by one year feed only two meals a day, one of meat and one of cereal. Growing stock will eat more than when finally adult. German Shepherd Dog puppies grow on quickly but nothing should be done to make them grow too fast or problems will arise.

DIETS FOR ADULT GERMAN SHEPHERD DOGS

1.	Raw beef	1–1½ lb (454–680 g)	wholemeal bread 8 oz (227 g)	Mineral, vitamin supplement
	Raw tripe	1–1½ lb (454–680 g)	up to 8 oz (227 g) bread or biscuit	Mineral, vitamin supplement
2.	Tinned meat (Meat only)		up to 12 oz (340 g) biscuit meal	Mineral, vitamin supplement
	Tinned meat/ cereal mixed 1½ to 2 average cans	up to 8 oz (227 g)	biscuit meal	Mineral, vitamin supplement
	(Not recommended as a regular diet)			
3.	Complete foods expanded semi moist (Rough guides)	20 oz (567 g) 20 oz (567 g)		

All the complete-food manufacturers will provide details of their products. Makers directions must be followed.

now considered a necessary supplement for the growing dog). Kelp (seaweed powder) is a good source of minerals. Every effort should be made to provide the dog with suitable bones to gnaw. On no account should cooked chicken bones be given to a dog.

The main thing is to give the dog a diet suitable for his way of life, one that will keep him fit and not overweight or too thin.

Any change of diet should be done slowly, a little of the new food being added as the same amount of old food that the dog is used to is removed.

A cat and dog life!

GROOMING

The German Shepherd Dog has an easy coat to maintain but needs a regular brush. When doing a full moult he will need more attention and a stiff brush and a metal comb will help to shed the dense undercoat. He should seldom need a bath.

Whilst grooming he should be examined for fleas and treated with a suitable remedy when necessary. If he is exercised where ticks are likely to be picked up, they must be removed at once. Look at his mouth, teeth, eyes and ears. Check his toe nails as well because these may not get worn down enough with exercise and have to be cut back which will require a visit to the veterinary surgery. This all-over handling of the dog is an important part of grooming because if treatment is necessary at any time he will not mind being examined. He should enjoy his daily grooming.

It's important to check teeth regularly

A dog's life…

USEFUL ADDRESSES

The Kennel Club, 1 Clarges Street, London W1Y 8AB
(For details of breed and training clubs, obedience, working and agility trials, regulations, registration, transfers and Standard of Points of the Breed.)

The British Veterinary Association, 7 Mansfield Street, London W1M 0AT
(For details of the KC/BVA Hip and Elbow Dysplasia Schemes)

The British Association of Homoeopathic Veterinary Surgeons, Alternative Veterinary Medicine Centre, Chinham House, Stanford in the Vale, Faringdon, Oxon SN7 8NQ

The American Kennel Club, 4th Floor, 260 Madison Avenue, New York NY 10016/2401

ACKNOWLEDGEMENTS

The author is most grateful to the following for permission to reproduce copyright photographs in this book: J. Cree; D. Cullum; V. Egger; A. Forrest-Byrne; R. Freeman; Guide Dogs for the Blind Association; G. Gwestyn-Pryce; M. James; J. Legg; P. Meaton; Carla Niewenhuizen; J. Oliver; Steph (Mrs S. Holbrook); K. Stevens; A. Vickerman; Messrs. Cullen, Dolphin, Tisdale, Traylor and Witty.

Dedication

To Lulu, the grey sable who introduced me to the German Shepherd Dog and to all those who have helped me learn about this wonderful breed.

British Library Cataloguing-in-Publication Data.
A catalogue record for this book is available from the British Library

ISBN 0.85131.773.1

Published in Great Britain in 2000 by
J. A. Allen an imprint of Robert Hale Ltd.,
Clerkenwell House, 45–47 Clerkenwell Green,
London EC1R 0HT

Series design by Paul Saunders, layout by Terence Caven
Series editor John Beaton
Colour processing by Tenon & Polert Colour Scanning Ltd., Hong Kong
Printed in Hong Kong by Dah Hua International Printing Press Co. Ltd.